THE TRAINER'S POCKETBOOK

11th Edition

By John Townsend

Illustrations by Phil Hailstone

"As always, this new edition of the Trainer's Pocketbook is a must-have resource for any trainer. The new additions are insightful and complete an already indispensable guide to training practice. I love it!"
Fabio Grassi, Executive Learning Director, IMI, Ireland

Published by:
Management Pocketbooks Ltd
Laurel House, Station Approach, Alresford, Hants SO24 9JH, U.K.
Tel: +44 (0)1962 735573 Fax: +44 (0)1962 733637
Email: sales@pocketbook.co.uk
Website: www.pocketbook.co.uk

Previous ISBN number 978 1 903776 16 2
This eleventh edition published 2013 ISBN number 978 1 906610 54 8

E-book ISBN 978 1 908284 31 0

British Library Cataloguing-in-Publication Data – A catalogue record for this book is available from the British Library.

Design, typesetting and graphics by **efex ltd**.   Printed in U.K.

CONTENTS

AUTHOR'S PREFACE

Here I am again writing a preface to the Trainer's Pocketbook – this time to the 11th edition. On the surface, training may appear to have changed considerably since this book was first written, but the basic principles remain as true as ever.

So here is the new Trainer's Pocketbook. Bang up to date and still unashamedly for you the front-line trainers; who are training people in training rooms large or small, state of the art or frustratingly ill-equipped. Much of training nowadays is done, and done very well, online, but you're still out there in flesh and blood giving hands-on help to real people.

This new edition has been totally revised in light of the advances in training technology, especially in the audio-visual field, but retains all the still-valid classics that have made it a favourite with trainers all over the world for so many years. And in comes lots of fun interactive stuff you can do on the web in front of the class – dreams come true for veteran trainers like me!

I want to give special thanks to fellow pocketbook writer Paul Tizzard and to master trainer Derek Fox for their invaluable help in the updating process. Thanks too, as always, to Phil Hailstone for the new graphics.

Ours is a wonderful profession. We're dedicated to only one thing – helping people grow. Keep on helping!

John Townsend, Mas la Papesse, 2013

INTRODUCTION

3 DIMENSIONS TO TRAINING

Training is a valued and rewarding profession because it is dedicated to helping people grow. A Master Trainer's performance can be measured on three dimensions:

Subject matter, knowledge and experience

- Technical competence in subject matter(s)
- Practical 'on the job' experience
- Academic qualifications
- Knowledge of the training function
- Competence in promoting training

Trainer techniques and skills (design and delivery of training courses)

- Training needs analysis
- Applying learning theory to course design
- Keeping trainee recall high
- Making learning fun
- Performing (voice control, eye contact, body language, etc)
- Using audio-visual support
- Leading discussions
- Creating and conducting exercises
- Training evaluation

Concern and availability to facilitate learning

- Empathy
- Listening skills
- Asking and answering questions
- Dealing with 'difficult' trainees
- Facilitating
- Adapting style/content to fit trainees'needs

3D TRAINER GRID

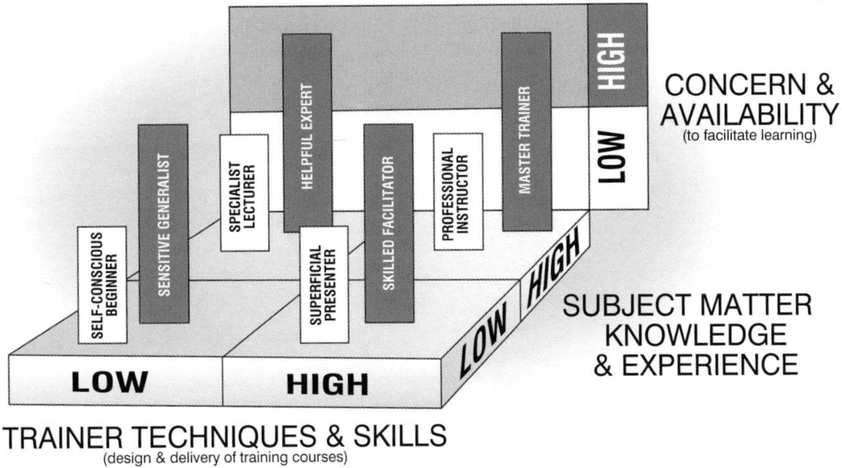

A 'Has-Been'

A 'Drip under pressure'

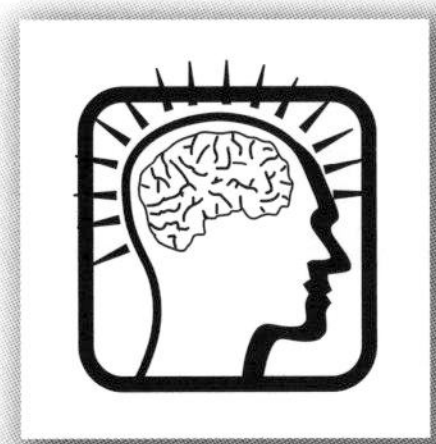

LEARNING THEORY

LEARNING THEORY

BRAINS

HOW ADULTS LEARN

- If they want and need to
- By linking learning to past, present or future experience
- By practising what they have been taught
- With help and guidance
- In an informal and non-threatening environment

BRAINS

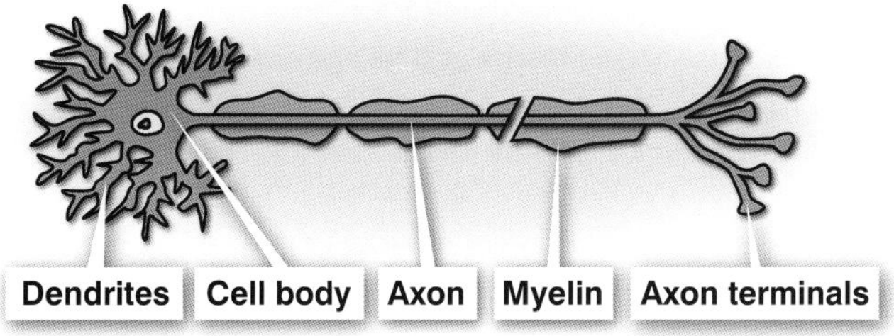

Neurologists are now saying that the average brain contains 100 billion brain cells (neurons). Each one is like a tiny tree with messages passing from branches to roots, each making hundreds of connections to other cells as we think. The total 'megabyte' capacity is inconceivably large.

BRAINS

DO BRAINS DECLINE?

The myth that brain power declines with age has finally been exploded.

- If the brain is stimulated **no matter at what age** new 'twigs' will grow on each brain cell's branches and increase the total number of possible connections
- Some of the world's most creative people have been exceptionally prolific at advanced ages (Gauguin, Michelangelo, Haydn, Picasso)
- We generate new brain connections more rapidly than the average loss of brain cells – even if we lose 10,000 brain cells a day from birth, the total number lost at age 80 would be less than 3%

BRAINS

SPEED/PREFERENCES

Neurologists have a lot to teach teachers and trainers! Dr. Patrick Georges' work in Belgium in the 1990s showed that:

- The average person can think at 800 words per minute but the average trainer can only talk at 120 wpm – **so we must give our participants something interesting to do with their spare 680 wpm!**
- The brain goes into 'auto shut-off' after only 10 minutes if it is not given something to stimulate it – **so we must vary the media and give multi-channel messages!**
- When a message is given once, the brain remembers 10% one year later; when it is given six times, recall rises to 90% – **so we must repeat, recap and review**
- The brain prefers: rounded diagrams and figures to square ones; Times and Helvetica typefaces; dark letters on light background; colour, colour, colour!!!

BRAINS

RETENTION: THE PROOF

It may be that our brains retain every piece of information they ever receive:

- **Death-type experiences:** people snatched from death say that their entire life flashed before them
- **Hypnosis:** under competent supervision hypnotees have unlocked vast memory banks
- **Surprise stimulation:** the 'déja vu' experience may be triggered by sights, sounds or smells
- **Experiments:** in experiments where patients received electrode treatment, they 're-lived' past, forgotten experiences
- **Mnemonics:** using special 'memory systems' normal people can rival famous stage magicians

LEARNING THEORY

BRAINS

RECALL: 5 MAIN FACTORS

F*IRST* — We are more likely to remember the beginning of events or the first in a series of events

R*EVIEWED* — Recall falls rapidly after 24 hours without review

O*UTSTANDING* — We remember unusual things exceedingly well!

L*INKED* — Recall is high for things which are linked by mnemonics or analogy

L*AST* — We are more likely to remember the end of events or the last in a series of events

The Finnish **FROLL**
(A cousin of the Norwegian Troll)

BRAINS

RECALL OVER TIME

BRAINS

HOW TO KEEP RECALL HIGH

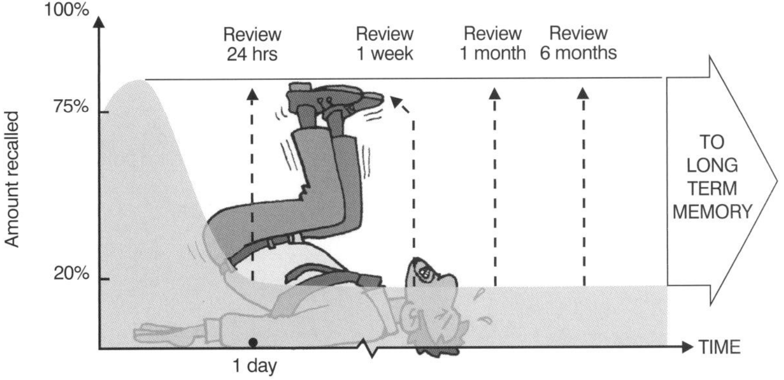

BRAINS

LOGIC V CREATIVITY

LOGICAL

- Speech
- Calculations
- Intellectual analysis
- Reading
- Writing
- Naming
- Ordering
- Sequencing
- Complex motor sequences
- Critique
- Evaluation
- Logic

CREATIVE

- Creativity (new combinations)
- Artistic activity
- Musical ability/Rhythm
- Emotions
- Recognition
- Comprehension
- Perception of abstract patterns
- Spatial abilities
- Facial expressions
- Holistic ability
- Intuition
- Images
- Colour

BRAINS

STIMULATING THE BRAIN

Professional trainers encourage learners to tap into their logical **and** creative skills. Experiments have shown that:

- People who have been trained to use one set of skills more than the other (eg accountants, engineers versus artists, musicians) find it difficult to 'switch' when necessary

- When the latent skills are stimulated and encouraged to co-operate with the stronger skills there is a greater synergy (1 + 1 = 5!)

Example: Newton understood the theory of gravity while day-dreaming

Applications: Trainers should combine analytical exercises with creative, expressive activities

BRAINS

VHF

To help trainees to use the full range of cognitive styles and functions we must remember that information is stored with **V**ery **H**igh **F**requency – in VHF!

***V**ISUAL*
- Pictures • Scenes • Images • Logos • Diagrams
- Graphs • Charts • Photos • Drawings

***H**EARING*
- Words • Music • Sounds • Accents
- Conversations

***F**EELING*
- Emotions • Smells • Tastes
- Tactile experiments • Pain/Comfort

BRAINS

MULTI-CHANNEL MESSAGES

Because people have different personalities and cognitive styles they store information in different ways, in the form of pictures (**V**), words (**H**) or sensations and feelings (**F**) so we, as professional trainers, must give **multi-channel messages.**

This means giving colourful visual back up to our verbal messages at the same time as appealing to trainees' emotions and senses.

These messages will be stored simultaneously in several parts of the brain and therefore multiply the chances of recall.

BRAINS

MNEMONICS

Many devices exist to help people recall multi-channel messages. The Germans call them 'donkey bridges' (Eselsbrücke) because they help the donkey of ignorance across the bridge to knowledge! They are **mnemonics** (memory devices) which **link together** two or more pieces of information. By linking together visual, hearing and/or feeling data, the donkey bridge creates a distinct and more memorable whole.
Example: the FROLL on page 15!

Note: A mnemonic (not newmonic!) is from a Greek word and means **any** kind of memory device, not just first letter acronyms.

BRAINS

DONKEY BRIDGES

Here are 5 kinds of donkey bridges which trainers can use to revolutionise trainee recall!

- **First Letter Acronym** (Flac!)
  Take the first letter of every word or phrase to be remembered and create a new word and (if possible) image
  Example: As a trainer you should **pamper** the audience with your voice by using pampers – **P**rojection **A**rticulation **M**odulation **P**ronunciation **E**nunciation **R**epetition **S**peed (see page 59)

- **First Letter Phrase** (Flep!)
  Create a phrase where each word begins with the letter of each thing to be remembered in a list
  Example: **R**ichard **O**f **Y**ork **G**ave **B**attle **I**n **V**ain to remember the colour sequence of **R**ed **O**range **Y**ellow **G**reen **B**lue **I**ndigo and **V**iolet in a rainbow

BRAINS

DONKEY BRIDGES

- **Sounds**
  Select music, songs or sound effects which will remind your trainees of your messages when they hear them in the future
  Examples: Use a 'polka' (POLCA) as the theme tune for a management course on **P**lanning **O**rganising **L**eading **C**ontrolling **A**chieving; Tina Turner's 'You're The Best' for a sales team course

- **Rhymes & Slogans**
  Create a memorable rhyme or slogan to 'anchor' your training message
  Examples: For a trainer it's 'Optional to be a professional'; Peace Corps water-saving slogan for the Caribbean: 'When it's yellow let it mellow, when it's brown, flush it down!'

- **Logos & Image Association** (Lima!)
  Design a logo for your course; create visual aids which help trainees remember key messages by associating them with a powerful picture – logos last longer!
  Example: Think of any flag or any company logo and reflect on all the messages this simple shape brings to your mind

MIND SET

However hard we try to keep trainee recall high, the enemy is **Mind Set**. When people hear or see something that clashes with their beliefs or values, they experience **Cognitive Dissonance**. Because of the discomfort caused by this dissonance, they will either justify their present beliefs/behaviour or distort the new information so that it no longer challenges their 'world view'. Some famous people have been victims of their mind set!

- 'Who the hell wants to hear actors talk?' (Harry Warner, 1927)
- 'There is no likelihood that man can ever tap the power of the atom' (Robert Millikan, Nobel Prize, 1923)
- 'Sensible and responsible women do not want to vote' (Grover Cleveland, 1927)
- 'Heavier-than-air flying machines are impossible' (Lord Kelvin, 1895)

MIND SET

Faced with inevitable and totally natural problems of mind set, we trainers must help our trainees to overcome the discomfort caused by cognitive dissonance. Like Shakespeare's Mark Antony, we must start from **their** point of view ('Brutus was an honourable man') and find a **WIFT** (**W**hat's **I**n it **F**or **T**hem?) to help them change their minds.

By concentrating on WIFTs we help them to justify changing their skills, knowledge or attitudes by providing a real need to do so.

Example: Faced with a salesperson whose mind set is 'I should be out selling, not listening to this nonsense', you should concentrate on how your course can help her sell more.

Exercises:

- Think of one of your own courses. What WIFTs can you think of for a 'dinosaur' trainee whose mind set is 'our present system has worked very well up to now'?
- How could you find WIFTs to overcome the following mind set:
  'What can this upstart teach **me**; s/he's half my age!'?

LEARNING ENVIRONMENT

THE IDEAL ENVIRONMENT

CHECKLIST

- Good audio visual equipment (see appropriate section)
- Appropriate seating patterns (pages 29 to 33)
- Comfortable chairs
- Good writing surface for each participant
- Thermostatically controlled temperature (ideal ambient temperature = 18° C)
- Independently controlled ventilation (air conditioning or windows)
- Good supply of refreshments
- Adequately sound-proofed room, with 5 square metres space per participant
- Natural daylight (windows with blinds/curtains), with minimum 500 lux lighting
- Central electrical commands (lights, audio visual, etc)

SEATING PATTERNS

'U' shape

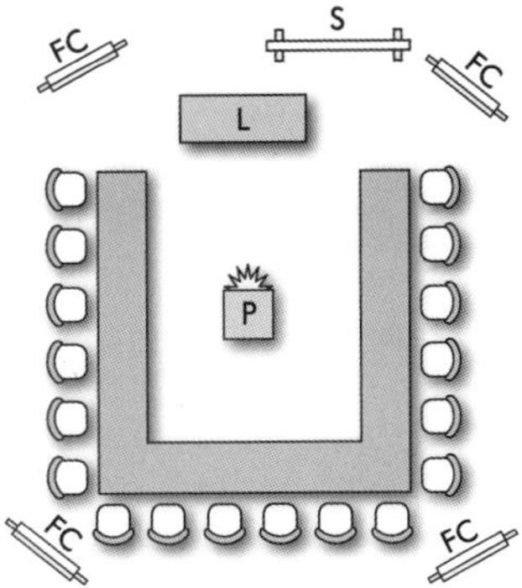

Advantages

- Businesslike
- Trainer can walk into 'U'
- Generally good participant visibility
- Standard, therefore non-threatening
- Subgroups can be formed (see FCs)

Disadvantages

- Somewhat formal; needs ice-breaking
- Some participants masked by audio visual equipment
- Front participants constantly at 60-90° (neck ache)
- Rear participants are far from screen/flip chart

FC = Flip Chart / P = Projector / S = Screen / L = Laptop/Tablet

SEATING PATTERNS

'V' shape

Advantages

- Best pattern for visibility/neck ache
- Optimum trainer/participant contact
- Less formal and intimidating than 'U'

Disadvantages

- Space requirements (only small groups)

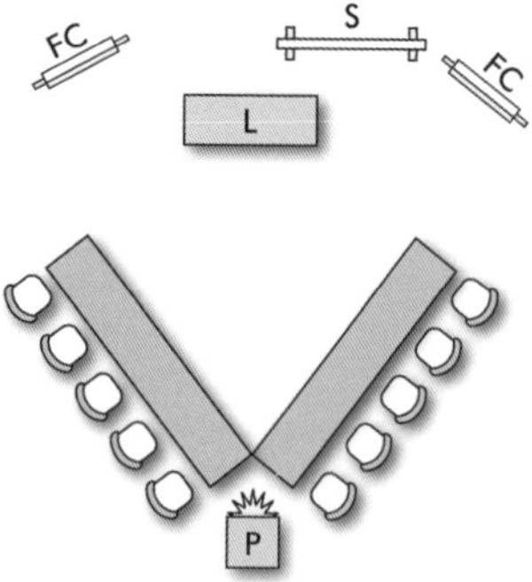

FC = Flip Chart / P = Projector / S = Screen / L = Laptop/Tablet

SEATING PATTERNS

Circle

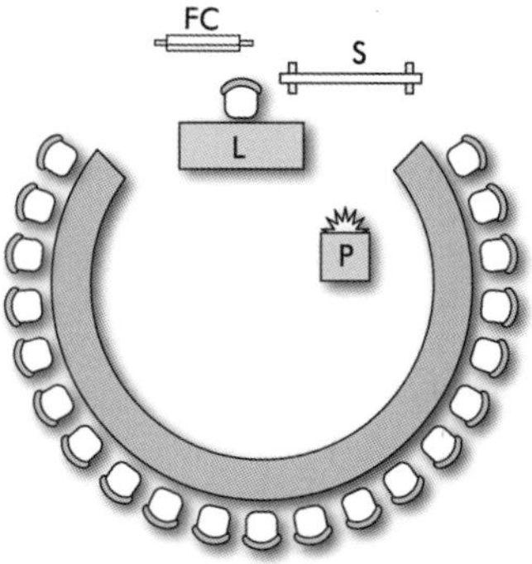

Advantages
- Ideal for sensitivity training sessions
- Encourages maximum participant involvement
- Excellent trainer/participant contact
- Minimum side conversations;
  no informal group formation

Disadvantages
- Difficult to find tables which can be set up in a circle
- Some participants have poor visibility/neck ache
- Without suitable tables participants may feel unnecessarily 'exposed'
- Overtones of 'touchy/feely' style encounter groups

FC = Flip Chart / P = Projector / S = Screen / L = Laptop/Tablet

SEATING PATTERNS

Amphitheatre

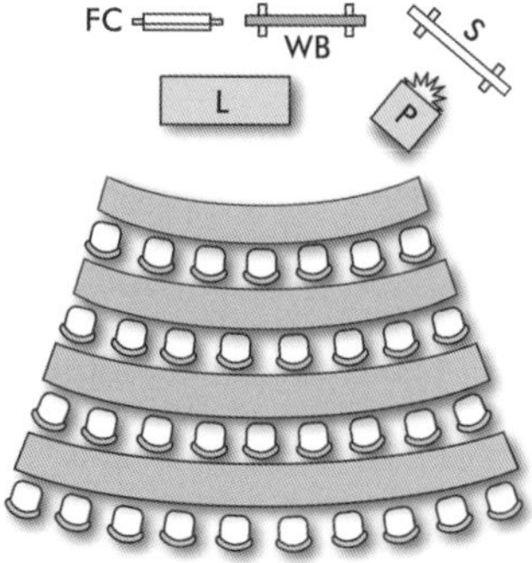

Advantages

- If room is well designed, excellent visibility and acoustics
- Very space-effective
- Good for lecture-type presentations

Disadvantages

- Very poor trainer/participant contact
- Difficult to set up unless room is designed with permanent seating
- Back rows must be elevated
- Very university-like

FC = Flip Chart / P = Projector / S = Screen / L = Laptop/Tablet / WB = Whiteboard

SEATING PATTERNS

All-in-one

Advantages

- Good for courses with many break-out sessions for groups
- Cost-effective (saves on break-out rooms)

Disadvantages

- Could be cramped
- Possible noise level problems

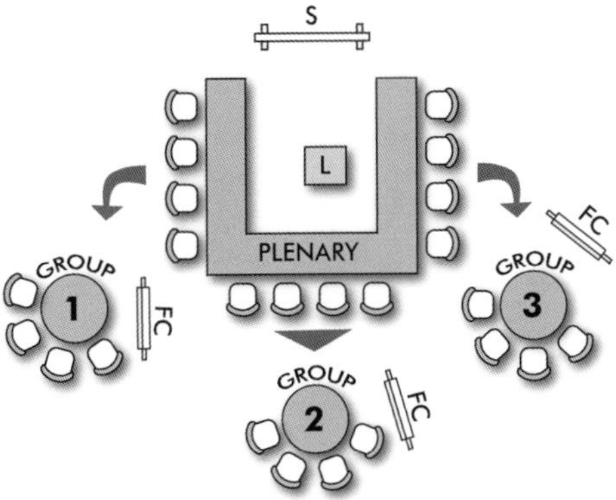

FC = Flip Chart / S = Screen / L = Laptop/Tablet

SEATING PATTERNS

PSYCHOLOGY

- Research shows that distance reduces participation – trainees in back rows are less likely to participate than those in front
- Any kind of 'row' reduces interaction: it is difficult for those in the back row to hear front row contributions and for those in the front row to twist round to interact with people behind
- Changes in seating patterns from one session to another can be psychologically upsetting for participants
- At repetitive sessions participants will invariably sit in the same place
- Angry or cynical participants will attempt to move away from a group seating pattern

SETTING UP THE ROOM

LEARNING ENVIRONMENT

MEDIA

VARYING THE MEDIA

As a general rule the learning environment should provide a change of pace/medium/subject/blood circulatory pattern every 10 minutes to avoid ‘auto shut-off’ (see page 13).

The professional trainer will, therefore, plan seminar coverage so that new audio-visual interventions, and new topics, come at fairly regular 10 minute intervals.

S/he will also plan for regular discussion periods, small group work or ‘stretch breaks’ to fight the descending learning curve.

Lastly, voice control (pitch, volume, modulation) can help change the pace of a seminar.

PREPARING TO TRAIN

PREPARING TO TRAIN

THE 5 W'S

QUESTIONS TO ASK

The success of a seminar, course or instructional module depends on a great number of variables. Before preparing yourself to train, you must answer five questions specifically – the five **W**'s!

***W**HY?*
- Ask why you are training at all. What are the trainees' objectives? What should trainees think or do at the end of the course?

***W**HAT?*
- Ask what you can put over in the available time. At what intellectual level will you pitch your teaching? What audio visual aids will you need?

***W**HO?*
- Analyse the trainee group: Age? Nationality? Level? Language abilities? Prior experience? Expectations? Mind set?

***W**HEN?*
- Ask whether the timing of the course is good for you and for them. Period of year? Weekdays/weekends? Morning? Afternoon? Evening?

***W**HERE?*
- Ask about and prepare for environment. Building? Room? Layout? Seating patterns? Interruptions? Temperature? Noise?

STRUCTURE

HOW TO DESIGN A LEARNING EXPERIENCE

B. GUNAR EDEG R.A.F. (B) *

The Icelandic pilot who joined the Royal Air Force ('B' Squadron)

* This mnemonic device has helped thousands of trainers all over the world to design more memorable and results-orientated training courses. For example, Richard Bradley from the Master Trainer Institute near Geneva, as well as teaching trainers how to use the model, also consults with major multinational organisations to create or re-design world class learning experiences for their employees.

STRUCTURE

DESIGN: STEP 1

***B*ANG**	• Always start with a learning 'hook' or attention-getter
***G*AP**	• Establish the gap between participants' present skills/knowledge and those to be acquired during the course
***U*NDERSTAND**	• Check that participants understand the existence and size of skills/knowledge gap
***N*EED**	• Establish the need for participants to close the skills/knowledge gap
***A*SK/ANSWER**	• Ask and answer questions to check participants' individual needs (encourage those with smaller gap/need to help with 'teaching')
***R*OUTE MAP**	• Outline course coverage, stressing results to be achieved (during and after the course) in closing skills/knowledge gap

STRUCTURE

DESIGN: STEP 2

***E**xplain*	• Explain each new skill/learning in digestible chunks using appropriate **V**isual, **H**earing and **F**eeling support (see page 82)
***D**emonstrate*	• Demonstrate skills and/or show how knowledge applies to them; use **VHF** support
***E**xercise*	• Allow participants to exercise each new skill or to feedback their understanding of new knowledge
***G**uide/correct*	• Show participants how well they have learned and correct any inadequacies

STRUCTURE

DESIGN: STEP 3

RECAP
- Review all learning points at end of each module (or beginning of next); use **VHF** support

ACTION PLAN
- Agree on an action plan for the transfer of new skills or knowledge to real life

FOLLOW-UP
- Agree on any follow-up or refresher

BANG
- Always finish with a succinct and provocative encapsulation of the learning experience

PREPARING TO TRAIN

MEMORY TECHNIQUES

NAME CARDS

Unless you are in a formal school setting, make sure that each participant is provided with a ready-made or do-it-yourself 'tent card' for his/her name. Ask for big bold letters so you can read the name from any part of the teaching area.

Tips *With cardboard tent cards, bend over a corner to keep the card from collapsing.*

Super tip from master trainer Derek Fox: Get participants to write key learning points onto the inside of their name cards and take them away at the end of the course.

COURSE TIMING

DOWN TIME

In a training day of 9 hours (08.30 – 17.30) always plan for down time as follows:

- Latecomers, settling, housekeeping = 10 mins
- Coffee/Tea breaks = 20 + 20 = 40 mins
  (even if you have planned 15 minute breaks!)
- Lunch and 're-settling' after lunch = 75 mins
  (even if you have planned 1 hour!)
- Stretch breaks, breaking into syndicates and other miscellaneous down time = 25 mins

Total = 2 hrs 30 mins

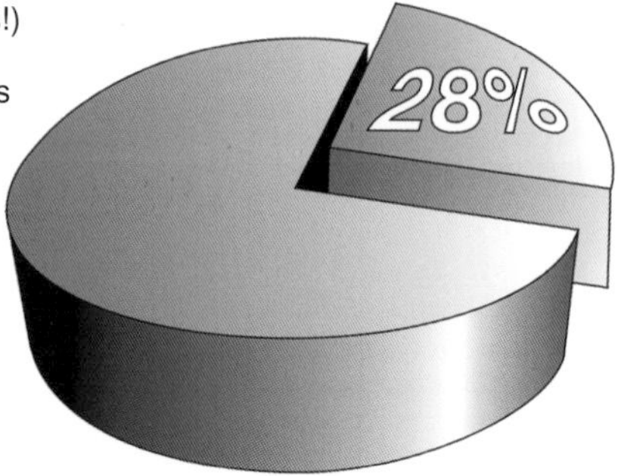

PREPARING TO TRAIN

COURSE TIMING

TIMING TIPS

- Always keep a clock or watch on your desk – but don't rely on looking at the watch on your wrist. Alternatively use your phone/tablet 'timer' app
- Use a chronometer or good kitchen timer for timing break-out sessions, separate modules, etc (especially if you've banned all phones, including your own)
- Always allow time for discussion – build it in to your course plan

TRAINING METHODS

EFFECTIVENESS OF DIFFERENT METHODS

Ranking of methods depending on TEACHING GOALS (1 = high, 8 = low)

METHOD	KNOWLEDGE ACQUISITION	ATTITUDE CHANGE	PROBLEM-SOLVING SKILLS	INTER-PERSONAL SKILLS	PARTICIPANT ACCEPTANCE	KNOWLEDGE RETENTION
CASE STUDY	4	5	1	5	1	4
WORKSHOP	1	3	4	4	5	2
LECTURE	8	7	7	8	7	3
SIMULATIONS	5	4	2	3	2	7
FILMS	6	6	8	6	4	5
PROGRAMMED INSTR.	3	8	6	7	8	1
ROLE-PLAYING	2	2	3	1	3	6

Source J. Newstrom "Evaluating Effectiveness of Training Methods"

TRAINER PREPARATION

- Always carry a checklist of material, equipment, etc, to the training room
- Arrive at the training room at least one hour before the start of the programme to prepare material and equipment
- Take at least 15 minutes from this time to prepare yourself:
  - physically; centring energy, grooming, posture and breathing
  - mentally; visualising the participant group, trying to imagine how they are feeling and asking/answering the question, 'How can I best **help** these people to change and grow, given the programme objectives and organisational culture?'
- Always prepare a trainer guide/mind map or training plan

TRAINER PREPARATION

PERSONAL STANDARDS

- Keep up-to-date yourself; your examples, your material, your media, your exercises
- Consciously manage personal energy levels by avoiding temptations to over-eat, over-drink or under-sleep before or during the programme
- Keep physically fit with at least one type of exercise per week

Training delivery

GENERAL

NAMES AND FACES

When faced with a room full of new trainees you will need to remember their names, but they don't need to know *how* you do it.

- Listen to name
- Spell it in your head
- Repeat name as often as possible during training event
- Look for an outstanding facial feature
- Exaggerate the feature
- Associate

  Carlo = imagine him driving a small car
  Gina = see her wearing jeans
  Jim = picture him on a running machine in the gym

This will ensure you can address (and impress) them during coffee break, lunch, etc.

ICEBREAKERS

Professional trainers always start with an **Icebreaker** or **Inclusion Activity** (see page 112 for some examples).

WHY?

- When trainees arrive in a training room they are usually a loose mix of individuals with different mind sets
- At the beginning of a course, trainees are usually **not** thinking about the trainer or the course content but about their neighbour, sights, sounds and smells in the room, coffee time for phoning/checking emails, the end of the day for errands, etc
- An inclusion activity will make them feel **included** and, if well designed, help them to relate to the others in the group; it can also provide a bridge into the course itself
- Above all it puts the spotlight on **them** (the most important people in the room) and takes it off **you** and allows you to relax into the course

ICEBREAKERS

WHAT?

A good inclusion activity should be:

Foolproof:	has been tested and works!
Amusing:	trainees should enjoy it
Bridged:	linked to the course subject (if possible)
Unique:	trainees should not have done it before
Lively:	has movement, exchange and chatter
Optimistic:	is positive and non-threatening
Uncomplicated:	is easy to explain and organise
Short:	lasts between 5 and 10 minutes

This donkey bridge (see page 22) was developed by Richard Hamilton and the 'Red Team' at a WWF Train the Trainer Course.

TRAINING DELIVERY

ENTHUSIASM

YOU GOTTA BELIEVE!

- If you're not enthusiastic about your subject, how can you expect the trainees to be!!
- Consciously use your eyes and eyebrows to communicate enthusiasm
- Always keep a sparkle in your voice
- Fight boredom of repetitive sessions by introducing new anecdotes, examples, etc, or by changing lesson structure
- Use the web! Keep them awake with YouTube, TED talks, Twitter, etc

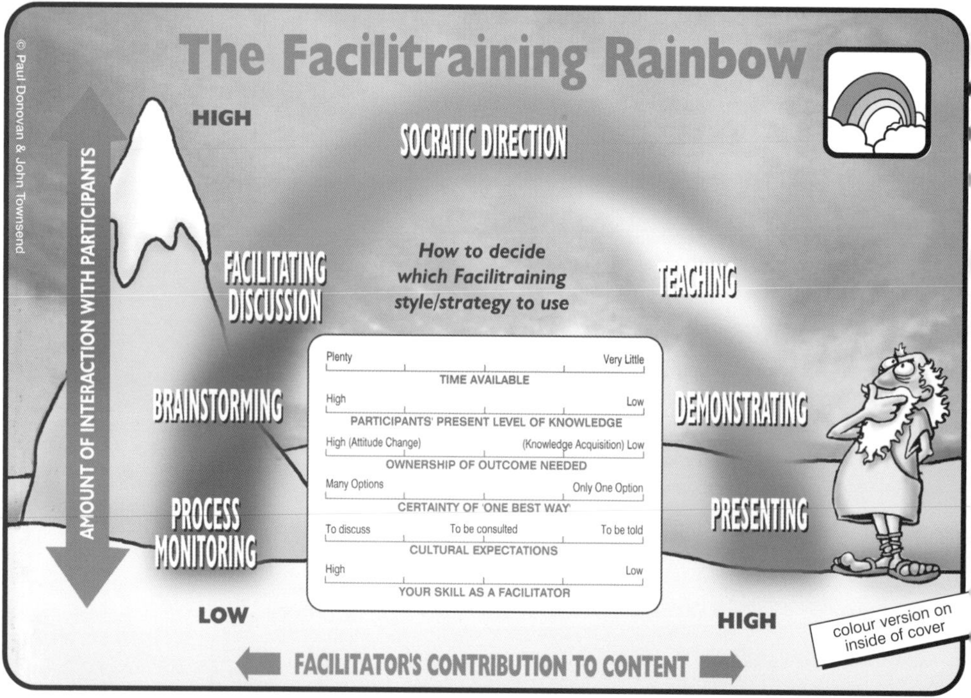

© Paul Donovan & John Townsend
The Facilitraining Rainbow
HIGH
SOCRATIC DIRECTION
FACILITATING DISCUSSION
How to decide which Facilitraining style/strategy to use
TEACHING
BRAINSTORMING
DEMONSTRATING
PROCESS MONITORING
PRESENTING
AMOUNT OF INTERACTION WITH PARTICIPANTS
Plenty
Very Little
TIME AVAILABLE
High
Low
PARTICIPANTS' PRESENT LEVEL OF KNOWLEDGE
High (Attitude Change)
(Knowledge Acquisition) Low
OWNERSHIP OF OUTCOME NEEDED
Many Options
Only One Option
CERTAINTY OF 'ONE BEST WAY'
To discuss
To be consulted
To be told
CULTURAL EXPECTATIONS
High
Low
YOUR SKILL AS A FACILITATOR
LOW
HIGH
FACILITATOR'S CONTRIBUTION TO CONTENT
colour version on inside of cover

THE FACILITRAINING RAINBOW

The Facilitraining Rainbow is a simple model to help trainers decide which style of training best suits which situation. The various criteria in the middle of the rainbow will help you determine whether to be more to the right of the rainbow (presenting mode) or more to the left (facilitating mode). Each of the seven styles, summarised below, combines varying amounts of interaction with participants, with the trainer's own input on content, and one blends into another as you 'surf' the rainbow.

PRESENTING (low interaction/high contribution)

The classic and often necessary style to put across information. However, as competition from the multimedia environment grows, trainers need to perform at an increasingly professional pitch so as not to be zapped by participants.

DEMONSTRATING (medium to low interaction/high contribution)

Not as 'one way' as presenting, demonstrating involves interaction with participants in as much as they are asked to try out in some way what has been presented.

THE FACILITRAINING RAINBOW

TEACHING (medium to high interaction/medium to high contribution)

When in the classic teaching mode, the trainer provides structured learning experiences and guides participants towards pre-determined learning objectives. He or she nevertheless provides some latitude for interpretation at an individual level.

SOCRATIC DIRECTION (high interaction/low to high contribution)

This is the 'maieutic' method pioneered by Socrates whereby the facilitrainer asks questions and then reformulates the answers as necessary to lead participants to a desired learning outcome. The rainbow provides for a wide range of 'leading' strategies from relatively open to relatively closed. The common element in all Socratic styles is the amount of interaction. It is based on the premise that 'people don't argue with their own data' even when it is massaged and channelled towards a hidden learning outcome – as long as the 'facipulation' is done professionally and sincerely.

THE FACILITRAINING RAINBOW

FACILITATING DISCUSSION (medium to high interaction/low to medium contribution)

When using this style the facilitator interacts quite often with participants to invite opinions, control the process and give own opinions (if only to provoke more discussion).

BRAINSTORMING (low to medium interaction/low contribution)

Here the facilitator conducts a classic brainstorming session – interacting with participants only to encourage them to give their ideas but hardly ever evaluating or adding ideas.

PROCESS MONITORING (low interaction/low contribution)

As the 'guardian of the process' the facilitator makes no personal contribution to the content of the discussion but occasionally regulates the flow of participants' contributions according to a previously agreed set of process rules.

The next 14 pages look at the stages of the rainbow in more detail

PRESENTING / DEMONSTRATING

NERVES: THE MURPHY MONKEY

As you get up to speak, it's as if a monkey has suddenly jumped onto your shoulders. He claws your neck and weighs you down – making your knees feel weak and shaky. As you start to speak, he pulls at your vocal chords and dries up your saliva. He pushes your eyes to the floor, makes your arms feel 10 metres long and attaches a piece of elastic to your belt – pulling you back to the table or wall behind you!

Experienced speakers know about the Murphy monkey. Within the first 30 seconds they throw him to the audience! When you throw the monkey to one of the participants, suddenly the spotlight is on them and not on you. How ...?

- A question, a show of hands, a short 'icebreaker' (participant introductions, an exercise or quiz, etc) a discussion, a 'volunteer' or simply a reference to one or more of the participants – all these are ways of putting the monkey on **their** backs for a few moments

  This takes the pressure off you and gives you time to relax, smile and get ready to communicate your message loud and clear.

PRESENTING / DEMONSTRATING

USING YOUR VOICE

PROJECTION	Speak louder than usual; throw your voice to back of room
ARTICULATION	Don't swallow words. Beware of verbal 'tics'
MODULATION	Vary tone and pitch; be dramatic, confidential and/or triumphant
PRONUNCIATION	Watch tonic accents; check difficult words; beware of malapropisms
ENUNCIATION	Over emphasise. Accentuate syllables
REPETITION	Repeat key phrases with different vocal emphasis
SPEED	Use **fast** delivery to excite and stimulate; **slow** delivery to emphasise or dramatise

PRESENTING / DEMONSTRATING

GETTING ON THE RIGHT VHF CHANNEL

When you are presenting to a group, **words and facts are not enough**. You need to transmit your message in **VHF** – **V**isual, **H**earing and **F**eeling (see also page 20).

For the past 25 years I've been conducting an experiment into how much people remember from messages given on these three different 'channels'. So far, over 1000 people from all over the world have participated.

The subject matter for all three messages is Australia. The first, 'visual' message is a slide with five different pictures illustrating features of Australia (shown for one minute). The second, 'hearing' message consists of reading, in one minute, other interesting facts about Australia. The third, 'feeling' message is a one minute story with five facts about koala bears, read while passing round a furry toy koala bear doused with eucalyptus oil.

When tested 24 hours later on what they remember, average scores (out of 5) are:

- **3.9** for the 'visual' facts; **1.9** for the 'hearing' facts ; **4.2** for the 'feeling' facts

These are averages….a few people score well on the 'hearing' test, while most say something like *'as soon as you started reading I stopped listening!'*

PRESENTING / DEMONSTRATING

LIGHTHOUSE TECHNIQUE

Sweep the audience with your eyes, staying only 2-3 seconds on each person – unless in dialogue.

This will give each participant the impression that you are speaking to him/her personally and ensure attention, in the same way as the lighthouse keeps you awake by its regular sweeping flash of light.
Above all, avoid looking at one (friendly-looking) member of the audience or at a fixed (non-threatening) point on the wall or floor.

TRAINING DELIVERY

PRESENTING / DEMONSTRATING

TYPES OF BODY LANGUAGE

POSTURES/GESTURES	• How do you use hand gestures? Sitting position? Stance?
EYE CONTACT	• How's your 'Lighthouse'?
ORIENTATION	• How do you position yourself in class?
PROXIMITY	• How close do you sit/stand to participants?
LOOKS/APPEARANCE	• Are looks/appearance/dress important?
EXPRESSIONS OF EMOTION	• Are you using facial expressions to express emotion?

PRESENTING / DEMONSTRATING

BODY LANGUAGE TIPS

- Don't be tempted by manual props (pens, pointers, spectacles, etc)
- Don't keep loose change in your pocket
- Be aware of your verbal tics and work on eliminating them (ie: 'OK!' – 'You know' – 'and so forth' – 'Now ...')
- Watch out for furniture!
- Avoid 'closed' or tense body positions
- Don't worry about pacing, leaning, etc
- Check your hair/tie/trousers/dress before standing up!

PRESENTING / DEMONSTRATING

BODY LANGUAGE: HANDS

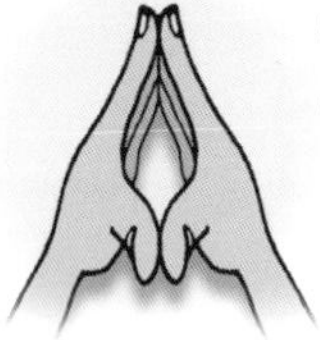

STEEPLING

- Self-confidence (intellectual arrogance)

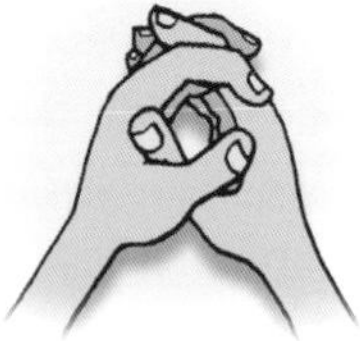

HAND CLASP

- Anxious, controlled

NOSE TOUCH

- Doubt

'L' CHIN REST

- Critical evaluation

MOUTH BLOCK

- Resisting speech

TRAINING DELIVERY

PRESENTING / DEMONSTRATING

BODY LANGUAGE: STANDING

THUMBS OUT
- In charge, dominant

FIG LEAF
- Self-control, tense

ARMS OUT
- Open, sincere, conciliatory

TABLE LEAN
- Authoritative, involved

LEAN ON
- Unthreatened, casual belongingness

TEACHING/SOCRATIC DIRECTION

Take a tip from the Ancient Greeks.

If you wish to encourage audience participation to prove a point use **Socratic Direction.**

K now the answers you want

O pen questioning technique

P araphrase participants' answers

S ummarise contributions (flip chart?)

A dd your own points

TEACHING/SOCRATIC DIRECTION

QUESTIONING SKILLS

Closed Questions – 'Who can tell me on which date?'
– 'Which/what specifically?'

Open Questions

- 'About' – 'How do you feel about ...?'
- Reflective – 'You don't feel comfortable with ...?'
- Hypothetical – 'What do you think would happen if ...?'
- Framing – 'Help me to see how this fits with ...?'
- Silence – ....?
- Statements – 'Rosemary, you look as if you wanted to say something'

Always avoid: Multiple – a string of questions
Leading – 'Don't you think it would be better to ...?'

Always allow participants 6-8 seconds to reflect and respond

TEACHING/SOCRATIC DIRECTION

LUBRICATORS

Verbal

- 'I see'
- 'Ah, ah'
- 'That's interesting!'
- 'Really?'
- 'Go on!'
- 'Tell me more about that'

Non-Verbal

- Nodding
- Constant eye contact
- Leaning forward
- Stepping aside
- Raising eyebrows
- Frowning (encourages clarification)

FACILITATING DISCUSSION/BRAINSTORMING

'B'ING

Here are four ways to keep a group discussion going:

- **BUILDING** Build on incomplete answers by adding own comments and asking for agreement or disagreement
- **BOOSTING** Support timid participants' contributions, boost their confidence and ask for extra comment
- **BLOCKING** Interrupt dominant/talkative/aggressive participants by asking what others think
- **BANTERING** Establish non-threatening atmosphere by engaging in friendly repartee with outgoing participants

FACILITATING DISCUSSION/BRAINSTORMING

BRAINSTORMING

A technique for obtaining ideas from a group. Here's how:

***A**SK*	Ask for/provoke ideas; if necessary wait 45 seconds before giving own
***R**ECORD*	Write **all** ideas on a flip chart (number them for future reference) – don't evaluate 'til end
***T**RIGGER*	Use 'B'ing discussion techniques to encourage participants to trigger ideas
***S**UMMARISE*	Summarise and/or regroup ideas; help group to choose best

PROCESS MONITORING

Just about every time you run an exercise you are 'process monitoring'. There is low interaction with participants (they are working more or less on their own) and low contribution from you as to content and outcome (the essence of learning by doing).

The facilitrainer's attitudes and beliefs play an important part in being a good process monitor. Do you really believe that people learn by practising? Can you show them respect by leaving them to discover how to do something on their own, while monitoring only that they are sticking to the structure of the exercises and resisting the temptation to give them the answers too soon?

DEALING WITH DIFFICULT QUESTIONS

REFLECT/DEFLECT

Most participant questions are not questions. They are requests for the spotlight. If it's one of those rare, closed **real** questions – answer it succinctly. If not, first:

- **REFLECT** back to the questioner what you thought was the question ('If I understand correctly, you're asking ...')

Depending on how the questioner 'reformulates' the question, answer it, **OR**

- **DEFLECT** it as follows:
  - **Group** : 'How do the rest of the group feel?'
    : 'Has anyone else had a similar problem?'
  - **Ricochet** : (to one participant) 'Bill, you're an expert on this?'
  - **Reverse** : (back to questioner) 'You've obviously done some thinking on this. What's **your** view?'

DEALING WITH 'OUTBURSTS'

ACTIVE LISTENING

Whenever a participant interrupts or responds emotionally during a course s/he is probably overstating his or her feelings in order to justify the 'outburst'. In **every** such case use Active Listening. Never attempt to counter, argue, defend or take sides.

1. Take the outburst as a positive contribution (smile, encourage, nod, use lubricators).
2. Successively reflect back to the participant (in the form of questions) what feelings you heard being expressed. 'You're upset with ...?' 'You're unhappy about ...?' 'You feel that we should ...?' Active listening has three advantages:

   - You show the participant you're interested and not defensive
   - You allow the participant to confirm that what you heard was what s/he meant **or** to correct your interpretation
   - You quickly lead the participant to specify the **exact** problem and to suggest a solution

DEALING WITH CHALLENGERS

1. The Heckler

- Probably insecure
- Gets satisfaction from needling
- Aggressive and argumentative

What to do:

- Never get upset
- Find merit, express agreement, move on
- Wait for a mis-statement of fact and then throw it out to the group for correction

DEALING WITH CHALLENGERS

2. The Talker/Know All

- An 'eager beaver'/chatterbox
- A show-off
- Well-informed and anxious to show it

What to do:

- Wait 'til he/she takes a breath, thank, refocus and move on
- Slow him/her down with a tough question
- Jump in and ask for group to comment

DEALING WITH CHALLENGERS

3. The Griper

- Feels 'hard done by'
- Probably has a pet 'peeve'
- Will use you as scapegoat

What to do:

- Get him/her to be specific
- Show that the purpose of your presentation is to be positive and constructive
- Use peer pressure

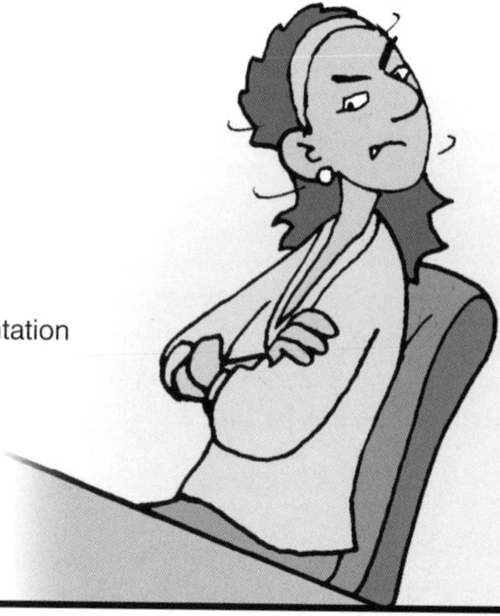

DEALING WITH CHALLENGERS

4. **The Whisperers** (There's only one; the other is the 'whisperee'!)

- Don't understand what's going on – clarifying or translating
- Sharing anecdotes triggered by your presentation
- Bored, mischievous or hypercritical (unusual)

What to do:

- Stop talking, wait for them to look up and 'non-verbally' ask for their permission to continue
- Use 'lighthouse' technique

DEALING WITH CHALLENGERS

5. The Silent One

- Timid, insecure, shy
- Bored, indifferent
- Disengaged

What to do:

- Timid? Ask easy questions; boost his/her ego in discussing answer; refer to by name when giving examples; bolster confidence
- Bored? Ask tough questions; refer to by name as someone who 'surely knows that ...'; use as helper in exercises

DEALING WITH CHALLENGERS

PSYCHOLOGICAL JUDO

(when classical methods have not worked!)

In physical judo you use the energy of your opponent to cause his downfall by changing your 'push' into 'pull'. In psychological judo you ask the difficult participants to be **even more** difficult. This gives them even more of the spotlight and attention than they wanted and they will use their energy to 'pull back' to avoid ridicule or overkill.

Classical Confrontation

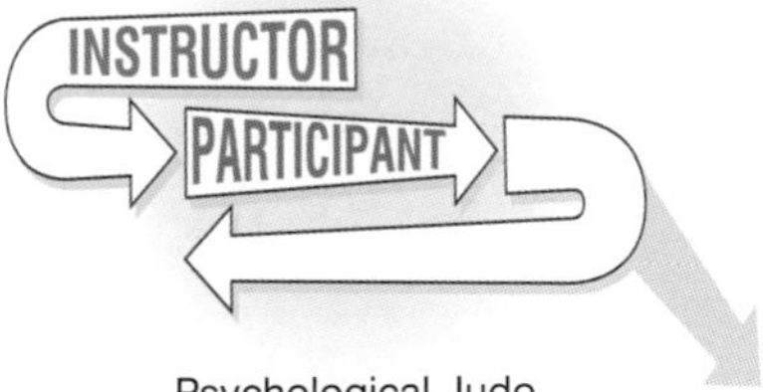

Psychological Judo

* See next page for examples

DEALING WITH CHALLENGERS

PSYCHOLOGICAL JUDO

Examples:

1 The Heckler — Appoint as class 'devil's advocate'. Insist that s/he criticises **whenever** s/he feels you are leading class astray. Demand negative remarks.

2 The Know-All — Agree with and amplify 'know-all' contributions. Ask for expert judgement when none is forthcoming. Get him/her up front to teach short module. Refer constantly to their expertise in subject matter taught.

3 The Griper — Ask for written list of gripes to help class maintain sense of realism. Get him/her to read list at end of day. Add to list whenever possible!

4 The Whisperers — State that time is short and ask those who don't understand not to interrupt but to ask their neighbour!

5 The Silent One — State that some people are shy and dare not participate. This does not mean they have not understood. Encourage shy ones not to participate.

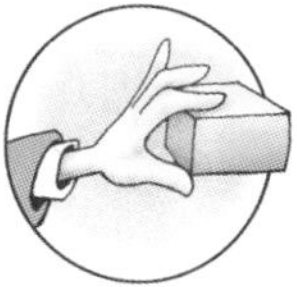

AUDIO VISUAL SUPPORT

How to use Visual, Hearing and Feeling support

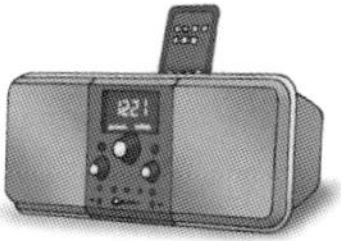

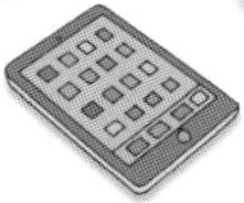

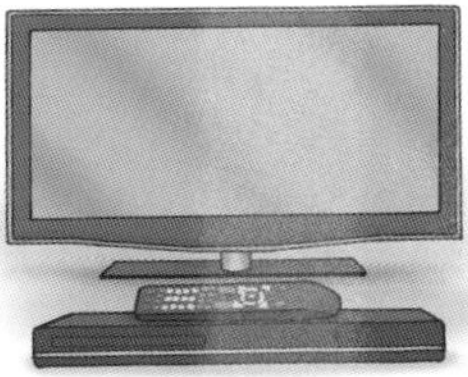

VHF COMMUNICATION

The human brain stores information in VHF – as Visual, Hearing or Feeling data.

Each participant has a preferred channel for remembering data. In my on-going classroom experiment on recall, 51% of participants say that their memory favours visual information, while only 7% prefer words/lectures and sounds. An astonishing 42% say they remember feelings, tastes, smells and tactile experiences best.

In order to 'tune in' to the maximum number of participants' wavelengths, professional speakers use a wide range of transmitters!

V • Imaging • Flip chart • Pinboard • Whiteboard • PowerPoint slides including video clips – YouTube, TED Talks, etc • Props and accessories • Word pictures

H • Music (instant access for changes of mood/illustrations) • Sound effects • Audio gimmicks • Onomatopoeia

F • Music (emotion/mood setting) • Handouts • Verbal descriptions • Anecdotes • Metaphors • Parables • Smells • Tastes • Cross-sensing

Feelings stay longer than facts!

AUDIO VISUAL SUPPORT

FIRST AID KIT

MASKING TAPE
(for sticking UP flips/ posters and sticking DOWN dangerous wires)

TIMER

THICK COLOURED MARKERS
(dry wipe and permanent)

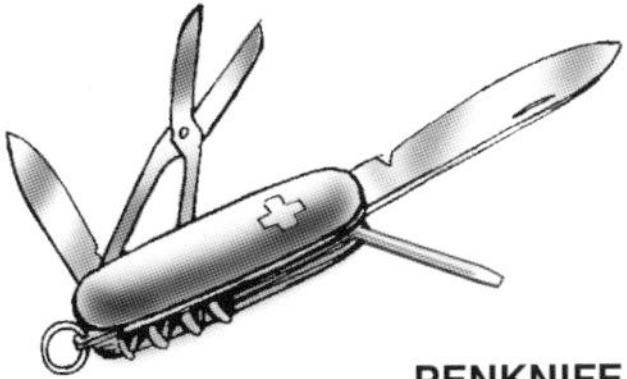

PENKNIFE
(for all the things you didn't think of)

BLU-TACK

AUDIO VISUAL SUPPORT

V : VISTIPS

GOLDEN RULES

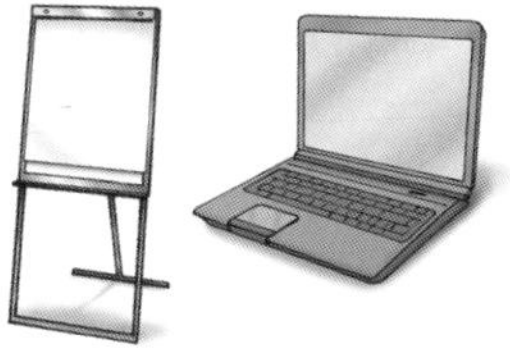

F*RAME*
- Use a standard **frame** for all visuals
- Create a **logo** or numbering system

L*ETTERS*
- Use **LARGE, LEGIBLE LETTERS**
- WORDS ARE NOT VISUALS
- Text 30-50 pts
- Titles 70-100 pts

I*MAGES*
- Use at least one **IMAGE/LOGO/GRAPH** on every visual

C*OLOUR*
- Use at least **one colour** more than black on every visual

K*ISS*
- **K**eep it short and simple!
- **1** topic. Bullet points and key words
- **S**ix lines maximum
- **S**ix words per line maximum

V : THE FLIP CHART

Despite (or maybe because of) the constant presence of hi-tech, all singing, all dancing PowerPoint software and internet access (see pages 91 – 100), the good old three-legged faithful friend, the flip chart is **increasing** in popularity with trainers in front of small- to medium-sized audiences.

Why?

- Portable (unlike most projection screens)
- Can be pre-prepared
- Intimate and less formal
- Generative – can be created on the spot, especially with audience input
- FRIENDLY!

AUDIO VISUAL SUPPORT

V : FLIP TIPS

PREPARATION

INVISIBLE OUTLINE

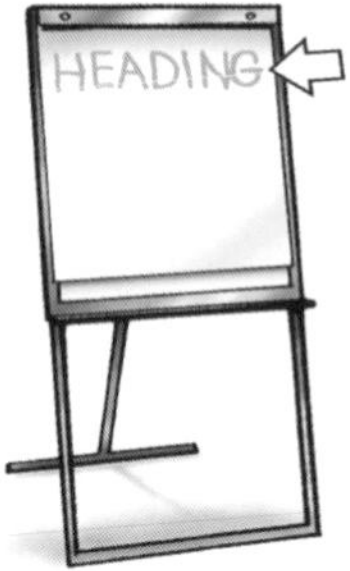

Lightly pencil in headings in advance when unsure of space, drawing, handwriting etc

CORNER CRIB

Use the top corner to pencil in your notes for each chart. Write small and no one will notice!

READY-MADE

Prepare key charts in advance

AUDIO VISUAL SUPPORT

V : FLIP TIPS

GRAPHICS

ATTRACTIVE

- Give each flip a title
- Use bullet points (like the ones on this page)
- Use at least two dark colours

BIG & BOLD

- Use **thick** markers (bring your own!)
- Should be legible from 10 metres!

CAPITAL KEY WORDS

- Never write sentences!

AUDIO VISUAL SUPPORT

V : FLIP TIPS

GRAPHICS

Whenever possible, use **cartoons** or **drawings** to personalise and add interest to your headings.

AUDIO VISUAL SUPPORT

V : FLIP TIPS

GRAPHICS

Standing

Every time you turn your back on the audience your voice and their attention disappear.

Since you can't write and face the audience at the same time (unless you are a contortionist!) you should:

- Write (a few words/seconds)
- Turn and talk
- Write (a few words/seconds)
- Turn and talk

V : GRAPHICS

AUDIO VISUAL SUPPORT

V : HEALTH WARNING!

VISUAL VALIUM

Just about every visual aid I've ever seen during a training course seems to have been designed to send me to sleep – a kind of visual Valium.

Too many words; too busy; no attempt to use space properly; no images; little or no colour. After a couple, I simply can't keep my eyes open.

Unfortunately, with the advent of presentations software they've become worse! Now they are professionally bad! Despite what your corporate identity programme might say, even a well-designed information slide becomes sleep-inducing when the same design is used over and over for different messages.

V : HEALTH WARNING!

At a recent conference I counted the words and/or numbers on every professional looking slide shown by every particularly unprofessional speaker!

For the 37 slides shown by one earnest presenter, the average per slide was 95 words or figures. The overall conference average was 76 words per slide.

And almost every speaker read almost every one of them! Some of them said, *'You can't read this but what it says is...'* and then proceeded to read them to us. Some just turned to the screen and read them. Some tried but couldn't read them, so we had to try on our own while they talked about something else!

AUDIO VISUAL SUPPORT

V : SLIDE TIPS

AVOID SLIDING INTO THE PITFALLS

- **KISAP Keep It Simple And Punchy!**
- Remember – just because something is technically clever or easy to access, that doesn't necessarily make it good VISUALLY
- Beware of 'blinding them with science'.....I've seen potentially great course presentations ruined by technical overkill or failure to have a backup plan when technology lets you down
- Use the **FLICK** golden rules from page 84

AUDIO VISUAL SUPPORT

V : SLIDE TIPS

GRAPHICS & VIDEO

- **Clip Art:** Import your own pictures/ photos/ cartoons etc into a PowerPoint presentation or get them from the clip art library or the web
- **Animations:** Use PowerPoint's 50 or so 'animations' to give a 'movie' effect to your visuals – but don't overdo it! People may soon get fed up with text or clip art whizzing about just for the sake of it
- **Video:** Embed video clips directly into your presentation through 'Insert' and then 'Movie'
- **Sounds:** Go to 'Custom Animation' in PowerPoint to add sounds to text or object movement, or add your own sound bites

For more information check out: **www.presentationhelper.co.uk**

AUDIO VISUAL SUPPORT

V : SLIDE TIPS

GRAPHIC/CLIP ART

- Example of a slide illustrating that wood burning stoves in Kenya save $25 million a year and help fight deforestation.

AUDIO VISUAL SUPPORT

V : SLIDE TIPS

GRAPHIC/CLIP ART

- Example of a slide from a financial course, likening the function to a ship's sonar.

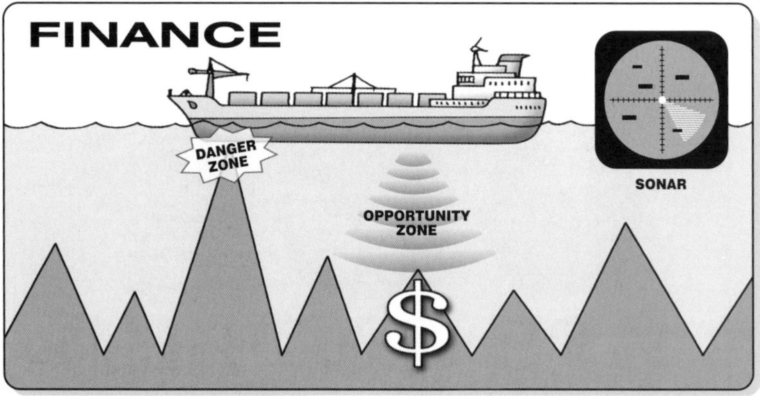

AUDIO VISUAL SUPPORT

V : SLIDE TIPS

USING THE WEB

Print Screen: A really simple way to get web pages and other internet illustrations into your course presentations is to use the Print Screen feature on your PC.
(Press Print Screen/ SysRq then cut and paste into PowerPoint)

'Live' Web Pages: With wifi in most training rooms now, you can go 'live' to a website. Set things up so that you can get to the page you want quickly. Black out the projector until you have the page ready to show. The longer you take to get there the more restless the trainees will become.

A good website to check out is:
www.pptfaq.com

AUDIO VISUAL SUPPORT

V : SLIDE TIPS

USING A WEBCAM OR TABLET

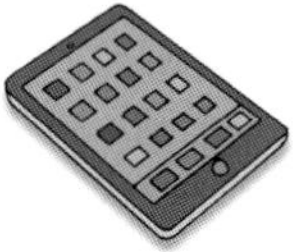

Interviews, messages and demonstrations
Add some live interest to your course presentation by bringing an absent colleague or expert into the training room for a live interview or demo of something via a webcam, or a tablet with its built-in camera.

Examples:
A brief Q&A session with the HR Director on a new policy
An important message from the CEO
A demo of a new product by a technical person
An on-site report from a sales person
A quick look at a new building with the facilities manager

Tips

Make sure you've briefed the 'on-camera' colleague to be prepared to wait on line for you to go live and, when the moment comes, try to make the link from what you're saying to the live picture seamless — like on the TV news. Murphy's law (if it can go wrong, it will) is particularly applicable to this process!

AUDIO VISUAL SUPPORT

V : CREATING YOUR OWN VIDEOS

- Websites such as www.presentermedia.com allow you to design high quality custom video clips in seconds
- If you'd like to create more sophisticated videos for training simulations or skill demonstrations go to www.xtranormal.com or www.reallusion.com/ crazytalk/
- You can turn your smart phone pictures and videos into training support movies with Quicki: http//www.qwiki.com/

AUDIO VISUAL SUPPORT

V : ON SCREEN INTERACTION IDEAS

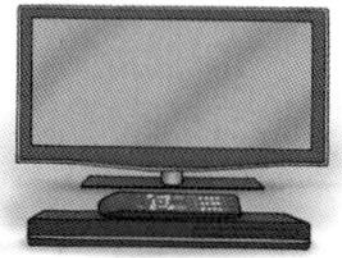

- Use **Twitter** in the training room – you can have live posts during the class in all sorts of feedback/ participant comment situations...the only limit is your imagination!
- Make 'mindmap' style **interactive presentations** with http://prezi.com/ or use pptplex plug-in for PowerPoint (this is available free from the Microsoft site)
- Create online **interactive question forums** to encourage participation/ test attitudes/ get consensus/ conduct 'surveys'
- Devise free **interactive stories** to get participants truly involved in the learning with http://writer.inklestudios.com/. You can create these stories to allow different options to be chosen at different steps in the narrative, leading to different outcomes. You write these outcomes to illustrate the consequences of making right/ wrong decisions in the use of the processes or skills you are teaching

V : THE WHITEBOARD

WRITING AND STICKING

Yes – whiteboards are still around and still going strong like the flip chart but, if used well, even more versatile for 'instant' course notes, quick demonstrations and dynamic illustrations of learning points.

Write on!

- Replaces blackboard (school memories)
- Great for brainstorming
- Change colour often
- Only use appropriate whiteboard pens

Stick up!

- Use 'Post-it' stickers to create group-work summaries (key phrases only); stick on whiteboard
- Move stickers into columns or categories; use pens to draw bubbles round salient groupings or to make links between stickers

AUDIO VISUAL SUPPORT

V : THE TALKING WALL

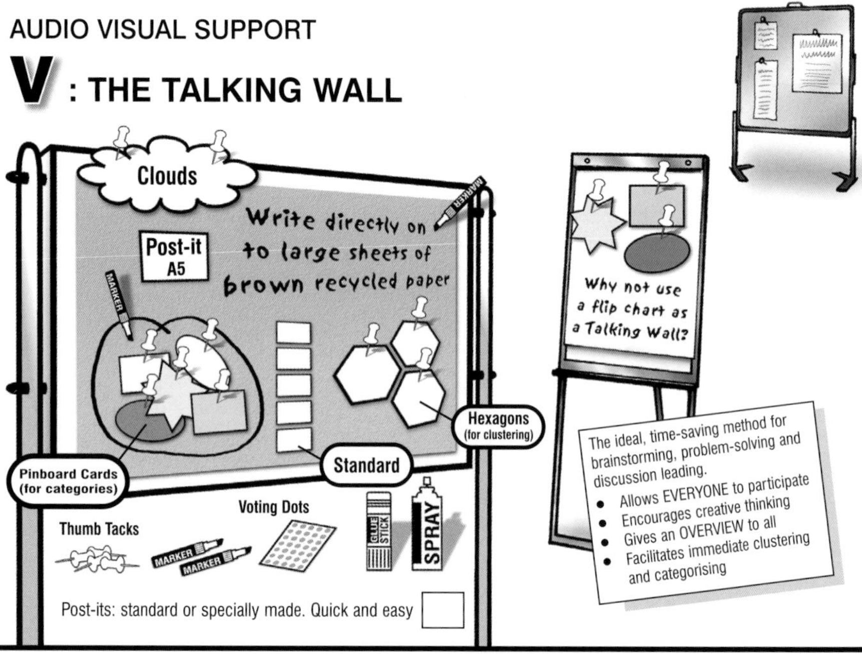

The ideal, time-saving method for brainstorming, problem-solving and discussion leading.

- Allows EVERYONE to participate
- Encourages creative thinking
- Gives an OVERVIEW to all
- Facilitates immediate clustering and categorising

H: USING MUSIC AND SOUND EFFECTS

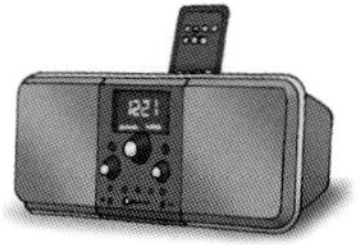

Here are some ways you should be using recorded music in your training course:

- To create a friendly atmosphere at the beginning of the course as participants come in, meet each other and settle down
- As background music during coffee breaks/intervals
- As an introductory 'bang'
- To create specific atmospheres for special messages (film music, theme tunes, sound effects etc)
- To illustrate a point amusingly with a song 'snippet' (example for a course on customer service: 'Help', 'Keep the customer satisfied', 'You can't always get what you want' etc). Use 'oldies but goodies', to appeal to a majority

NB You can either take your MP3 player and speakers to the training room, **or** incorporate the sound bites in your PowerPoint presentation (see page 94) **or** simply use your laptop as a music centre. Make sure you check music licence rules.

AUDIO VISUAL SUPPORT

H: THE MP3 PLAYER/ TABLET

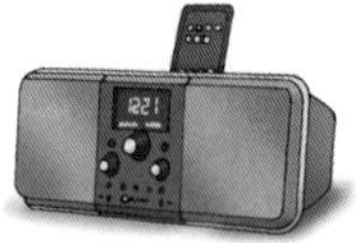

RECORDED SPEECH

Recorded speech can be useful for:

- Illustrating messages (salesman-customer, boss-subordinate)
- Examples of opinions (market research interviews etc)
- Bringing an absent colleague to the course
- Interjecting humorous anecdotes
- Giving examples of current radio adverts/trends

Why not record your session so you can work on your mistakes.

Tip *When recording audio examples, make sure you leave very little space between each recording. In this way you can press the 'pause' button at the end of one example, knowing that the next recording is cued to start as soon as you next hit the button.*

AUDIO VISUAL SUPPORT

F : ANECDOTES AND METAPHORS

'F' is for Feelings and sensations! 42% of people say that their memories favour this kind of information and, when tested, the same people remember 80% of facts given while 'appealing to feeling' the previous day.

- **ANECDOTES** are true stories which give 'live' examples of what's being presented and help people remember the message. For instance:
  - 'I recall we had one manager who…'
  - 'Someone was working with this software last week and…'
- **METAPHORS** are comparisons/analogies/similes which illustrate what is being presented by comparing it to something very visual or more easily recognisable/understood. They usually start with the phrase, 'It's a bit like…'

Example: the financial controller's sonar on page 96

AUDIO VISUAL SUPPORT

F : PARABLES

Parables persuade! They take away the defensive reaction we tend to provoke in participants when we ask them to change the way they do things. Parables (like the 'Prodigal Son') refer to a third party in a 'far away' place and thus feel safe. The participant, nevertheless, connects with the message and projects it onto him/herself which allows SELF-INITIATED change to take place.

AUDIO VISUAL SUPPORT

F : TOUCH, TASTE AND SMELL

TOUCH

Your audience will remember your key points much more clearly if they are INVOLVED. One way to ensure involvement is to give them something to touch. Handouts, samples, models, free gifts – all will help participants to participate and, therefore, remember.

TASTE AND SMELL

On the face of it, it would seem highly inappropriate for you, as a trainer, to ask your participants to taste or smell something! But… think about candy and air fresheners which could simply lend atmosphere to your course and maybe even help link your message to something pleasant in the participants' minds. Even if you don't actually produce smoke in your 'Fire Hazards' course or give them some coffee in your 'HR Services' session, you can always DESCRIBE tastes and smells!

F : CROSS-SENSING

If you'd like to hypnotise your audience, do some 'cross-sensing'! This simply means describing something in a way which appeals to all the senses: SIGHT, HEARING, TOUCH, TASTE, SMELL, HEAT/COLD/PAIN/EMOTIONS.

A manager for a large multinational held her sales audience spellbound for 10 minutes as she described how a magnetic resonance scanner worked by taking them into a hospital in their minds. Some participants reported that they were actually able to feel what it was like to be inside the scanner.

MURPHY'S LAW

'If something can go wrong – it will!'

O'Connor's corollary:
'Murphy was an optimist!'

The only way to beat Murphy is to be a professional and use the 3 P's:

- **Preparation**
- **Preparation**
- **Preparation**

VIDEO FEEDBACK

Here's an idea to help you accelerate your improvement as a trainer:

Record yourself giving part of one of your next training sessions (remember to ask the audience's permission) and then play it back at home.

Give yourself five objectives to work on for your NEXT course

GROUP & INDIVIDUAL EXERCISES

ICEBREAKERS

Here are **3** ideas for 'inclusion activities' (see pages 51 & 52) to supplement the classic 'please introduce yourself/your neighbour' presentations.

- **2 True, one False**
  Participants introduce themselves by giving one incorrect and two correct pieces of information about their background; likes and dislikes; present job, etc – the group must guess which is true and which false
- **Famous Pairs**
  Write the names of some famous pairs on post-its (Romeo/Juliet, Laurel/Hardy, etc) and stick them at random on participants' backs so they can't see who they are; they must then locate their 'partner' by asking others questions about their identity – these questions may only be answered by Yes or No
- **Stick-up Needs**
  Ask each participant to write 1-3 objectives for attending the course on separate post-its/ cards and to stick them on a flip chart or pinboard while explaining to the others; alternatively, you can collect the cards and stick them up – asking for comments as you do so

 Further icebreakers are available in the *Icebreakers Pocketbook* by Paul Tizzard & Alan Evans

THE QUIZ

In training courses where facts must be learned it is essential to 'exercise' participants' new knowledge. Written tests are fine but remind people of their school days.

A well-devised quiz will appeal and test at the same time.

Suggestions

- Break group into quiz teams to provoke competition
- Invent different categories of questions (like TV game shows)
- Keep scores on imaginatively designed board (whiteboard/pinwall)
- Don't forget the prizes!

CASE STUDIES

Case Studies

Concisely written, practical and realistic case studies will induce thinking, analysis, pro and con discussion and genuine efforts to find solutions to problems. Case studies help participants to apply theoretical knowledge to real-life situations and also serve as 'pace-changers' to stimulate interest and attention.

Case Study Rules for Trainers

- Know the facts of case study well
- Have pre-prepared questions to guide trainees during their own analysis of the facts
- Tabulate consensus items during discussion
- Encourage differences of opinion to explore alternative solutions
- The trainer should use Socratic Direction (see page 66) to summarise learning points from the case study

GROUP & INDIVIDUAL EXERCISES

VIDEO RECORDING

Nowadays video cameras are idiot and almost Murphy-proof! Recording trainees in individual or group practice sessions is a very powerful teaching tool!

TIPS

- Use a digital camcorder for easy access to recorded tracks
- Prepare connections to the TV monitor in advance to avoid delay
- Use fast forward during playback to save time
- If you have the equipment, record separate individuals/groups on different tapes/DVDs and split into sub groups for playback

People are hyper-sensitive about seeing themselves on video. First reactions of trainees who are not used to the medium concern their **hairstyle**, their **weight** and their **accent**.
Even when they accept their **look** and **sound** they may over-react with self-criticism and become depressed or defensive.

⇨ Always accept these reactions with sympathy and sensitivity, and stress confidentiality. Use professional feedback technique (see page 117)

ROLE-PLAYING

Role-playing

Role-playing is a dramatised form of case study in which trainees act out a human relations problem under the guidance of the trainer who elicits an evaluation of the performance in light of previously taught principles.

Pre-requisites for a successful role-playing exercise:

- The role play situation must be realistic
- The situation must be one with which participants can identify; characters should be of a type that really exists in the organisation
- Participants must live their parts
- Role-playing should not represent a threat to timid participants
- Trainer should play the 'challenger' role

Role-playing is not play acting. It is 'reality practice'.

ROLE-PLAYING FEEDBACK RULES

1. First ask role-player(s) for an 'auto-critique'.
2. Ask group to take notes and watch the video re-play (where appropriate).
3. Ask the group to give feedback.

Rules

- Always separate 'motivational' from 'developmental' feedback
- For developmental feedback, use the conditional tense and always offer an alternative (ie: 'I think it would have been more effective if you had ...')
- Always address the individual concerned and say 'you' not 'he/she'

PROJECT WORK

Projects

In modular courses and seminars, given at regular intervals, (weekly, monthly, etc) project work between sessions provides an ideal bridging, learning and review experience.

1. **Tailor-made** As a trainer you should develop relevant project structures which will allow trainees to practise each session's learning points – if possible in groups of 4-7.

2. **Canned** Many video-based packages exist which provide inter-session project work as an integral part of the course.

PROJECT WORK

THE GROUP RECAP

One kind of project worth highlighting is the group recap.

In courses which last more than one day, split the group into small teams and ask a different team to make a resumé of the previous day's learning at the start of each new day.

Teams invariably vie with one another to make **their** resumé the best (at least the most amusing), a lot of learning takes place and a good time is had by all (especially the trainer who has one less module to present!).

3 UNIVERSAL EXERCISE DESIGNS

CROSSWORDS

Crossword puzzles are a great way to help participants practise or recap recent learning.

It's relatively easy to create your own crossword for a knowledge test and even easier if you use a free crossword-making site like www.eclipsecrossword.com.

If you're going to 'do it yourself' then first think of 10-15 learning points you'd like to emphasise with one word answers. Plot these answers into a classic crossword format of numbered squares, tweaking them so that there's always an overlapping letter in the 'across' and 'down' lines.

Next, think of reasonably challenging questions which will provide each answer and print them at the bottom of the crossword sheet as clues (separating across and down clues).

Tip *If you can make large enough copies of your crossword, try getting groups to complete them in a competition and award a prize to the first group to get the puzzle right.*

3 UNIVERSAL EXERCISE DESIGNS

FOUR CORNERS

This exercise can be used when you are teaching a course which has any piece of learning that can be divided into four sections (4 Types of Leadership, 4 Steps to XYZ, 4 Learning Styles, 4 New Products, etc). Simply place a flip chart or, better still a large pinboard, in each corner of the training room and write the name of one of the sections on each.

Divide the group into four teams and assign them to a corner. Give them 10-20 minutes to write everything they can think of that they've learned about that section – as creatively and as colourfully as possible. At the end of the allotted time ask each of the teams to 'visit' each other's boards and note down questions they may have for their colleagues. Facilitate a plenary session where teams (still standing in their corners!) answer the questions.

> Remember... 'they who teach also learn!'

3 UNIVERSAL EXERCISE DESIGNS

CLUSTERCARDS

Clustercards are card-based learning puzzles for groups of 2-5 participants.

Choose something you teach that has a number of related steps, phases or types. These may be either sequential (like the four steps in a sales call) or ‘stand-alone’ (for instance six categories of customer/ product/ intervention…) Create a set of 3-4 cards describing each of these steps, phases or types plus a differently designed ‘title’ card for each. Get small groups to lay out the cards, with the correct ones under each title and, if applicable, in the right order.

EXAMPLE: Make four cards describing each of the FORM, STORM, NORM, PERFORM phases of team development as well as the four ‘title’ cards ie a total of 20 cards. Ask the groups to work together to place each of the four descriptive cards under their appropriate heading. See which team can finish first!

CONCLUSION

Well, that's it. Over 400 tips, tools and techniques in 124 succinct pages – hopefully practising what the Pocketbooks' philosophy preaches!

I've often been asked what the most important things are that I've learned in my career as a trainer of trainers so here, in summary, are a few key lessons that stand out:

Show them the Need and create the Want. Always respect the fact that the trainees are actually there! Generally speaking, people have something better to do with their brains than to sit and listen to you. They can only learn if they need and/or want to. So your job is to show them why they need to learn and help them want to do so by making the learning experience streamlined, lively and interesting.

Words are not Visuals. So many so-called visuals are useless. Word slides are like visual Valium. PowerPoint Prozac just sends them to sleep. Make your visuals visual and keep them to a punchy minimum.

CONCLUSION

Keep appealing to feeling. People like stories, they learn from emotion, they remember what has touched them and what they have touched. So, give examples, make technical subjects human and bring excitement into the training room with sights, sounds and sensations.

It's optional to be a professional. You **can** get away with sloppy preparation; you don't have to arrive at the training room an hour early. There's always a good excuse for not having the handouts ready, for not setting up the music or revising your course notes or checking participants' backgrounds. They probably won't walk out if you don't. It's optional to be a professional – or is it?

People don't argue with their own data. Take a tip from Socrates and ask questions – whenever possible get them to discover the answers for themselves.

Make every course a 'rainbow surfing' adventure. Lastly, have another look at the Facilitraining Rainbow on the inside covers and make a mental note to move left and surf! In other words, lecture as little as possible, vary your training style as much as possible and, above all .... **ENJOY YOURSELF!**

About the Author

John Townsend, BA MA MCIPD
John has built a reputation internationally as a leading trainer of trainers. He is founder of the highly-regarded Master Trainer Institute, a total learning facility located just outside Geneva which draws trainers and facilitators from around the world. He set up the Institute after 30 years' experience in international consulting and human resources management positions in the UK, France, the United States and Switzerland – notably as a European Director of Executive development with GTE in Geneva where he had training responsibility for over 800 managers in 15 countries. During his long career as a trainer of trainers he has not only helped to spread the unique Master Trainer Institute philosophy across the world via his conferences, seminars and bestselling training videos, but also written a number of widely translated management and professional guides.

Many thanks to Richard Bradley of the Master Trainer Institute for helping these tips and techniques come alive in the Management courses for participants from all over the world.
You can contact Richard at: Richard@mastertrainer.ch or www.mt-institute.com